Why Science Matters

Understanding Health and Behavior

Ann Fullick

Heinemann Library
Chicago, Illinois

Customer Service 888-454-2279
Visit our website at www.heinemannraintree.com

Editorial: Andrew Farrow, Megan Cotugno, and Harriet Milles
Design: Steven Mead and Q2A Creative Solutions
Illustrations: Gordon Hurden
Picture research: Ruth Blair
Production: Alison Parsons
Originated by Heinemann Library
Printed and bound in China by Leo Paper Products

ISBN: 978-1-4329-1840-8 (hc)
ISBN: 978-1-4329-1853-8 (pb)

13 12 11 10 09
10 9 8 7 6 5 4 3 2 1

Library of Congress Cataloging-in-Publication Data
Fullick, Ann, 1956-
 Understanding health and behavior / Ann Fullick.
   p. cm. -- (Why science matters)
 Includes bibliographical references and index.
 ISBN 978-1-4329-1840-8 (hc) -- ISBN 978-1-4329-1853-8 (pb)
 1. Human behavior. 2. Animal behavior. 3. Health behavior. I. Title.
 BF199.F85 2008
 150--dc22
                    2008014349

Acknowledgments
The publisher would like to thank the following for permission to reproduce photographs:
© Alamy **pp 11** (Wolfgang Kaehler), 13 (Steve Bloom Images), 22 (tbkmedia.de), 26 (Profimedia International s.r.o.), 31 (ImageState), 35 (Mike Goldwater), 35 (Christa Knijff), 38 (Megapress), 44 (Trevor Smith); © Barcroft Media **p 47**; © Corbis **pp 14** (Creasource), 17 (Roy Morsch), 18 (L. Clarke), 49 (David P Hall); © Corbis/Zefa **pp 27** (Gary Salter), 40 (Mika), 42 (Mika); © Digital Vision **p 23**; © FLPA/Konrad Wothe; Miden Pictures **p 23**; © Getty Images **pp 4** (Lars Klove Photo Service), 25 (Justin Sullivan), 29 (Nick White); © istockphoto.com **p 23**; © Istockphoto background image; © Nature Picture Library **p 20** (Pete Oxford); © Photolibrary/Oxford Scientific/TC Nature **p 33**; © Photolibrary/Phototake Science/Collection CNRI **p 36**; © Science Photo Library **pp 5, 7** (Wellcome Dept. of Imaging Neuroscience), 12 (Photo Researchers), 48 (BSIP VEM).

Cover image of an MRI brain scan reproduced with permission of © Getty Images/Photodisc. Background design reproduced with permission of © Istockphoto.

The publishers would like to thank Michael J. Reiss for his invaluable assistance in the preparation of this book.

Contents

Some words are printed in bold, **like this**. You can find out what they mean in the glossary.

Finding Out About Behavior

What is behavior?

Have you ever wondered why people behave the way they do? Some people always seem happy and content, while others are full of anger and **aggression**. Some people take drugs, drink too much alcohol, or eat so much that they become **obese**. There are people who love to exercise, and people who never move away from their television or computer screen.

The world around you is changing all the time, and the way you behave changes in response to your environment. The way people behave affects how they feel, and it also affects their health.

If you watch animals—your pets or animals in the wild—you will see that they have clear patterns of behavior. They react to hunger, and they respond to meeting other animals. In other words, they react to the world around them. In this book you will look at how the science you study in school can help you understand the way people and animals behave. You will find out how behavior affects health.

In scientific terms, behavior is defined as: The actions displayed by an organism in response to its environment. The scientific study of animal behavior is called **ethology**. Investigating animal behavior can happen in many different places, such as a laboratory, a zoological park, or the natural environment; from the depths of a rainforest, to a deserted piece of waste ground.

Humans and other animals behave very differently. Scientists can learn a lot by studying both!

Studying human behavior can be easier than studying other animals, because people can explain what they are doing and why. However, studying human behavior is full of difficulties and raises a lot of **ethical issues**. For example, it is not ethical to force humans to behave in a particular way for an experiment.

Lorenz and Tinbergen—the Fathers of Ethology

Scientists have observed animal behavior for many years. However, it was the work of Austrian biologist Konrad Lorenz and Dutch biologist Nikolaas (Niko) Tinbergen in the 1930s–60s that really developed the science of ethology.

Lorenz introduced many theories about how animal behavior patterns develop and the importance of **instinct**. Tinbergen produced evidence that supported Lorenz's ideas. Together they changed the way that animal behavior was studied. Lorenz's most famous work was with geese. He observed that shortly after hatching, goslings follow their mother everywhere. Lorenz showed that this is due to an instinctive behavior called imprinting. The goslings follow anything that moves and makes goose-like sounds. In the course of his research, Lorenz had many goslings imprinted on him (see photo above)! In 1973, Lorenz and Tinbergen were awarded the Nobel Prize in Physiology, or Medicine, for their work.

Responding to the environment

When you walk past a baker's shop, it is very tempting to buy, and eat, a cake or doughnut. When a male dog walks past a lamppost, he will likely sniff and urinate if given a chance. When the seasons change, birds take off and migrate to other countries, sometimes thousands of miles away. These examples of behavior are all responses to a change in the environment. How do we humans recognize that our surroundings have changed?

Sensitivity

All animals have some degree of **sensitivity**. Many animals have well-developed **sense organs**, which respond to changes in the world around them.

- Eyes respond to light, which makes it possible to see changes taking place. For example, someone may see a display of delicious cakes when passing a bakery.
- Ears are sensitive to sounds, making it possible to communicate with others and hear changes in the environment, such as an approaching car.
- The nose provides a sense of smell, which is particularly important to other animals, such as dogs. A lamppost carries hundreds of scent messages about other dogs that have visited the same place.
- Taste buds on the tongue provide a sense of taste, telling you if food is pleasant or not.
- Touch sensors in the skin provide information about the feel of the surroundings, for example whether a surface is soft, smooth, or prickly.

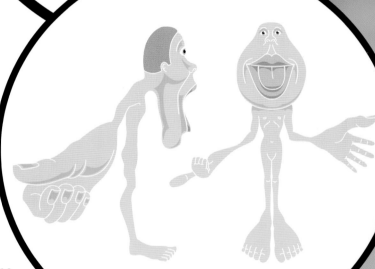

Different areas of the body have different numbers of sensory nerve endings. In this illustration, the enlarged areas of the body have a large number of sensory nerve endings. Sensory nerves send information about the world around you to the central nervous system. Then motor nerves carry the messages to the muscles, so you can act on that information.

The sense organs send electrical messages known as **nerve impulses** to the central nervous system. Depending on the type of animal, the central nervous system ranges from a simple tube to the complex brain and spinal cord of human beings. The information from the sense organs is sorted in the brain. Next, more impulses are sent out to stimulate the muscles of the body to move and respond.

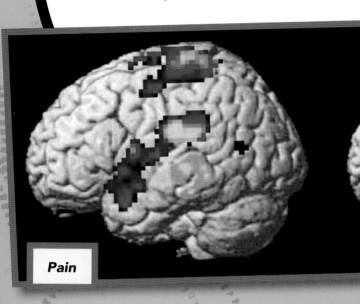

Empathy

Pain

The human brain is very complicated, but scientists are learning more and more about how it works from scans like these.

CUTTING EDGE: WATCHING THE BRAIN IN ACTION

MRI scanners allow researchers to see what is happening in the brains of animals, including humans. The scanners show which parts of the brain are active as we behave in different ways. A team of researchers from the United States have shown that when people feel rejected, the response in their brain is the same as though they were being physically hurt. It seems likely that this affects our behavior and makes us try to look after the people who are close to us.

The brain

The human brain is organized into different areas. Each area deals with different information and helps control the behavior of the body. The brain has some areas that control behavior without any conscious thought on your part. Other areas involve conscious thought, which allows you to have control over how you behave. Scientists still have a great deal to learn about the interactions between the brain and behavior.

Reflexes and simple behavior

If you put your hand on something hot or sharp, you pull it away before even thinking about it. This response is a reflex. Reflex actions are the basis of a lot of animal behavior. In humans, reflexes help keep you out of danger. They also control many of the basic functions of life, such as breathing and the contractions of your gut muscles. It would be very hard work if you had to remember to breathe every few seconds, and consciously make your gut squeeze the food through your body!

THE SCIENCE YOU LEARN: REFLEX ARCS

In a reflex, a **stimulus** is picked up by the sensory receptors. The nerve impulse travels through a sensory nerve to the central nervous system. It then travels through a "shortcut" straight back into the motor nerves. It travels on to the muscles, which contract and make your body react. This arrangement of nerves is called a reflex arc. Impulses also go up to your brain, so you know what has happened.

A reflex arc is a very rapid response to a change in the environment. It uses a reflective arc, which does not involve conscious thought.

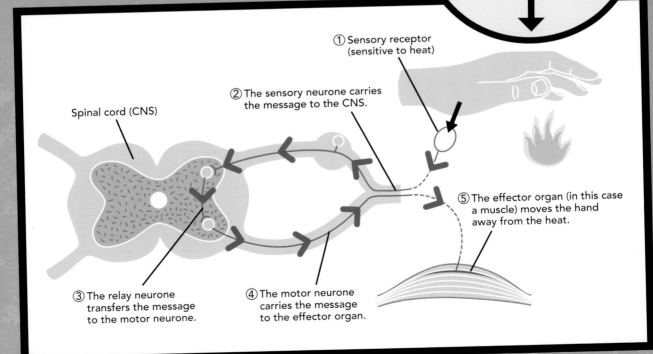

① Sensory receptor (sensitive to heat)

② The sensory neurone carries the message to the CNS.

Spinal cord (CNS)

⑤ The effector organ (in this case a muscle) moves the hand away from the heat.

③ The relay neurone transfers the message to the motor neurone.

④ The motor neurone carries the message to the effector organ.

Conditioned reflexes and learning

Reflexes like blinking are not learned. Instead, they are present from birth. Many other reflexes are learned, often without us realizing. These are called **conditioned reflexes**. For example, when a baby learns to walk it has to think about every step. Watch a small child walking. It is obvious that they have to concentrate on moving their legs, using their arms to balance and thinking about where to put their feet. Then watch older children or adults walking around. The action has become completely reflex, and there is no conscious thought involved at all.

If you have ever had a pet, from a dog to a goldfish, you will know that you can use external cues, or signals, to change their behavior. In other words, they can learn. When your dog sees you pick up the leash, it knows that signal means it is time for a walk, and the dog gets excited. When you touch the surface of the water, a goldfish knows it is time to be fed and comes to the top of the tank. This learning is often the result of developing conditioned reflexes.

CASE STUDY

Pavlov and His Dogs

In the late 19th and early 20th century, Russian scientist Ivan Pavlov set up a series of experiments with dogs. He showed that when dogs see their food, they start to produce saliva. Pavlov started ringing a bell just before he brought food to the dogs. After repeating this several times, the dogs would produce saliva when they heard the bell ring without seeing or smelling their food. They had learned to associate the bell with food, which is an example of learning through a conditioned reflex.

What drives behavior?

There are certain basic needs that drive behavior in all animals, from fish to humans. One of the most fundamental drives is for food. Hunger is behind many different levels of behavior. For example, carnivores eat other animals, so they have to catch their food. The behavior involved in catching food varies enormously. The larvae of ant lions dig circular pits in soil and then hide themselves at the bottom of the pits. When insects fall into the pits, the ant lion pounces and devours its prey. This hunting behavior is an instinct, which means that it is inherited behavior that is preprogrammed and does not need to be learned. All members of a species show the same pattern of instinctive behavior.

Lions—social hunters

African lions are social hunters. They work together as a team to surround and chase their prey. One lioness takes over from another until one is successful in bringing the prey down. Lion cubs have to learn how to hunt successfully. They have a number of instinctive behavior patterns that help. Cubs, like domestic kittens, pounce on moving things. They flatten themselves with their bodies low to the ground and creep up on their siblings (brothers and sisters). However, they need to watch the adults and learn how to interact to become part of a hunting pride (group).

Sand with your sweet potato?

Some animal feeding behavior is almost human. Scientists observed an amazing piece of behavior in a group of Japanese macaque monkeys. Tourists threw pieces of sweet potato from a boat onto a local beach to attract the macaques. The macaques collected the food and tried to brush the sand off. Then one young female started to wash her pieces of sweet potato in the sea to remove the gritty sand. The behavior quickly spread throughout the whole group. Only the adult males did not copy this behavior, although the young males soon followed their mothers and sisters!

Behavior on the move

One of the most dramatic animal behaviors is the mass migration of birds and mammals over thousands of miles. They travel in response to changes in the external environment, such as day length or temperature, or the need to reproduce. The migrations are almost completely instinctive. Some birds, such as geese, migrate for the first time in a family group and seem to learn the route. In other species, such as cuckoos, the young birds migrate independently right from the start.

Many animal behaviors involve temperature regulation. Insects and reptiles cannot control their own temperature using heat from the reactions in the body. They orientate themselves to make the most of the warmth of the early morning sun to heat themselves up and get moving. Later, as the temperature gets hotter and hotter, they move into the shade to avoid overheating.

Penguins can control their own body temperature internally, but live in such extreme conditions that they need to cluster together to conserve heat. These huddled chicks stand a much better chance of survival than if they stood alone.

Studying Behavior

Investigating animal behavior

Everyone knows something about how animals and humans behave because it is part of our everyday lives. To really understand behavior, scientists need to do more than watch their pet cat or observe their neighbors walking down the road.

Finding out how animals behave

Scientists have studied many different types of animal behavior, from courtship and mating to memory and learning. American psychologist Burrhus Frederic (B. F.) Skinner played a very important part in investigating animal behavior. He studied the way animals learn and invented the Skinner box. This box can be used to hold an animal, such as a pigeon or a rat. There is a button for the animal to press, a tray for it to receive a reward of food or water, and a way for the scientist to change the conditions. Skinner showed that animals learned new behaviors very quickly when they were rewarded. For example, pigeons could be taught to choose between a bright and a dim spot of light to get their reward.

A pigeon in a Skinner box soon learns what to do to get a reward of food.

Animals, such as rats and pigeons, are still used to study behavior in a laboratory. They are cheap and easy to look after. Most people do not object to scientists working with these small animals if they are treated in a humane way. However, animals in laboratory conditions may not behave in the same way as they would in their natural environments. Therefore, observations of animals in the wild are very important.

Jane Goodall and the Chimpanzees of Gombe

Chimpanzees are more like humans than any other animals. British **ethologist** Jane Goodall was one of the first people to carry out detailed research into chimpanzee family and social life. In the 1960s, she set up a long-term study of a group of chimpanzees at Gombe in Tanzania, Africa. She also helped American zoologist Dian Fossey, who set up a similar research project to study the behavior of mountain gorillas. German Professor Biruté Galdikas also worked with the great apes, studying orangutans. Observing apes in the wild gives scientists a way to **evaluate** the information they collect from animals in zoos and in laboratories.

THE SCIENCE YOU LEARN:
SCIENTIFIC INVESTIGATION

A chimpanzee uses a stick to fish for termites. Jane Goodall was the first person to report tool-making and tool-using in chimpanzees. Until then, everyone thought that only humans made tools.

In science lessons you learn how to form a hypothesis and test it using experiments. You must keep conditions the same and only change the factor you are investigating. You need to think about the accuracy and reliability of your evidence. Are your results similar to others in the class, or very different? Are they different because you are the only one who got it right, or is there a mistake in your method? Scientists studying behavior have to consider the same sort of problems. However, it is not easy to set up and control experiments on behavior, especially when they involve humans.

Investigating human behavior

To really understand human behavior, scientists need to observe people carefully. For example, newborn babies behave in similar ways all over the world. They sleep, stretch, cry, and soon start to smile. They have reflexes, including blinking and gripping tightly to anything placed in their hands.

In the same way, certain patterns of behavior are recognizable in all adults. However, there are far more differences in the way adult humans behave. This is true not just in different countries and communities, but even within the same family.

Internal factors

There are more than six billion people on Earth. Apart from identical twins, each one has a different set of genetic instructions. Although everyone is different, we all have a lot of genetic information in common. Some of that genetic information influences our behavior.

Humans have a number of behavior patterns that are inherited. These are called **innate** or instinctive behaviors. A lot of human behavior is built up as we learn from the responses to our innate behavior.

Some of the most basic aspects of human behavior are programmed into our genes and can be seen in very young babies.

For example, many facial expressions start off as innate. A newborn baby does not smile. Within a short time, a smile appears as an innate response to a pleasurable sensation, such as being cuddled by its parents. This smile immediately gets a very positive response from the parent. This reinforces the innate behavior, and the baby soon learns that a smile is a good way to get a lot of attention.

Personality also seems to have a strong genetic link. **Longitudinal studies** (a series of observations carried out on the same people over many years) have shown that some strong personality traits can be seen in very young children. Some children are easygoing and happy, others are more likely to cry and be sad. As the children grow, these basic personality types remain, although they may change depending on what happens to the children as they grow. In fact at least 50 percent of the way you behave is probably down to your **genes**. The rest is the result of external factors, and this is what makes us all so different.

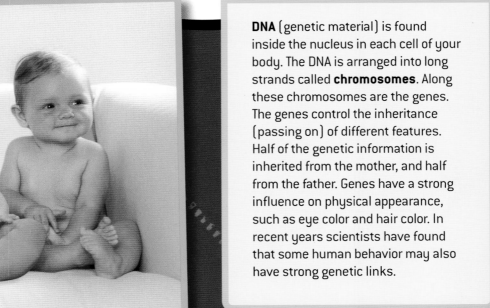

THE SCIENCE YOU LEARN: INHERITANCE AND GENETICS

DNA (genetic material) is found inside the nucleus in each cell of your body. The DNA is arranged into long strands called **chromosomes**. Along these chromosomes are the genes. The genes control the inheritance (passing on) of different features. Half of the genetic information is inherited from the mother, and half from the father. Genes have a strong influence on physical appearance, such as eye color and hair color. In recent years scientists have found that some human behavior may also have strong genetic links.

External factors and human behavior

Within each country and within each family, the external factors that affect human behavior differ. Even identical twins have different positions in the family and are treated slightly differently. What sort of external factors affect human behavior?

Bringing up baby

There is a lot of research that suggests that the way children are brought up affects their behavior throughout the rest of their lives. Most children are lucky enough to have parents who try their best as they raise their family. The idea of what is best varies among **cultures**, but if children feel valued and loved they will respond. Children need contact with other humans. Parents, siblings, grandparents, friends, and other caregivers—as well as the chance to try new experiences—all help children to develop healthy behavior patterns.

A child who is regularly beaten, or who sees other people hurt, is more likely to treat others badly. However, many children from harsh backgrounds make a great success of their lives and relationships. Children from "good" homes can behave in very destructive ways, turning to crime and drugs. So what else influences human behavior?

CUTTING EDGE: RESISTING PEER PRESSURE

Recent research at Nottingham University in the United Kingdom has shown that some teenagers have an advantage when it comes to resisting peer pressure. Many teenagers were shown pictures of angry young people. The teenagers' brains showed a lot of activity in the areas linked to getting information from the environment. In some of the teenagers, there was also a lot of activity in the area involved in decision making. These teenagers were less likely to be influenced by their friends.

From a very early age, children want to behave in the same way as their peer group. The approval of friends is very important.

Peer pressure

The influence of peers (group of people of a similar age with whom you spend a lot of time) has a big effect on the way humans behave. From an early age, children form like-minded groups. It can be very hard if a child does not fit in. Children are very quick to be unkind to others who are different. The importance of a peer group cannot be underestimated. If parents value education and want a child to succeed, but the child has a group of friends who think it is stupid to work hard at school, it is likely that the child's schoolwork will suffer. The child is not likely to give up the friends.

Peer pressure can be a great influence for good, or it can carry young people (and adults) into crime, alcohol, and drugs.

The environment also influences behavior. For example, it is not possible to spend hours in front of a television if you have to walk several miles every day to collect water. It is not easy to decide exactly what affects human behavior—there are a lot of factors to take into account.

Nature versus nurture?

For many years scientists have debated whether the way people behave is mainly the result of nature (their biology), or whether it is the result of nurture (the way they are brought up). At the moment, the evidence suggests that both are important.

It is possible to find out how a change in the environment—such as a lack of enough food, a loud noise, or overcrowding—affects behavior by setting up an experiment. Or an investigation can be set up to see whether reward or punishment encourages faster learning. However, care must be taken so that experiments are ethical, with no harm coming to animals.

It would be completely unethical to deprive babies of love to see if they behave differently. No one would be allowed to make humans live in very overcrowded conditions to see if they became more aggressive. It would be interesting to see if some humans have a genetic makeup that means they are more likely to become addicted to alcohol. However, it would be completely unacceptable to make a group of people drink large amounts of alcohol every day to see how many of them became addicted!

Overcoming the problems—twin studies

One way to overcome the problems of investigating human behavior is to look at evidence from large numbers of people. If this is combined with taking observations over a period of years, the results can be very reliable.

Identical twins are particularly useful for studying behavior because any differences in the way they behave must be due to nurture. Identical twins who have been separated from birth are most useful of all. Although this is relatively unusual, there are quite a few cases where it has happened.

When these twins are reunited, scientists can measure the similarities and differences between them. This provides real insight into which aspects of their behavior are inherited, and which are the result of the way they have been brought up.

The data below is based on a groundbreaking study carried out at the University of Chicago in 1937. The researchers looked at 50 pairs of identical twins raised together, 50 pairs of identical twins raised apart, 50 pairs of nonidentical twins, and 50 pairs of nontwin siblings. Some features, such as height, seem to be strongly genetic. Other features, such as mass, seem to be affected by nurture and behavior—for example, how much you eat. Intelligence seems to be a mixture—both inherited and affected by upbringing and opportunities.

Trait	Identical twins raised together	Identical twins raised apart	Nonidentical twins	Nontwin siblings
Height difference	1.7 cm (0.6 in.)	1.8 cm (0.7 in.)	4.4 cm (1.7 in.)	4.5 cm (1.8 in.)
Mass difference	1.9 kg (4.2 lbs)	4.5 kg (9.9 lbs)	4.6 kg (10.1 lbs)	4.7 kg (10.4 lbs)
IQ score difference	5.9	8.2	9.9	9.8

THE SCIENCE YOU LEARN: IDENTICAL TWINS

At the moment of conception, a sperm fertilizes an egg. The new cell, or zygote, starts to divide to form a baby. Sometimes, during the first few divisions, the ball of cells that forms the early embryo splits completely in two. Both groups of cells continue to grow and form two embryos with identical genetic information. The embryos continue to grow and develop to form genetically identical babies.

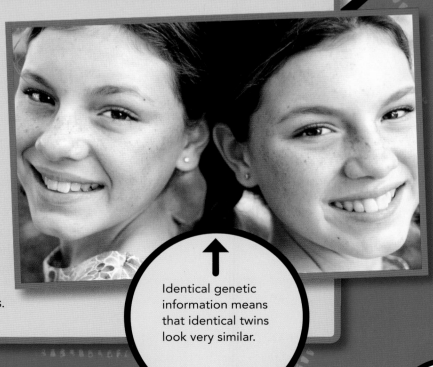

Identical genetic information means that identical twins look very similar.

The changing study of behavior

The way behavior is studied has changed over time. Many years ago it would have been unthinkable to consider animal behavior and human behavior together. Now it is recognized that we can learn a lot about how humans behave by looking at animals.

In the past, it was believed that you could tell whether someone was a criminal by measuring the lumps and bumps on their head! Now we understand that both genetics and the environment have an effect on behavior (see pages 18–19).

As our understanding of the causes of many diseases has grown, our knowledge of the links between behavior and health has also improved. It is well known that smoking cigarettes is linked to an increased risk of lung cancer and heart disease. Food choices affect health in the same way, as high-fat, high-calorie diets seem to be linked to obesity and heart disease.

Neuroscience, psychology, and psychiatry

The study of human behavior falls into several different groups:

Neuroscientists study the nervous system. They look at the structure, development, and function of the nervous system. They observe how diseases affect the brain. Studying the brain and the rest of the nervous system involves studying how humans behave. Activity in the nervous system usually shows up as behavior.

Psychology is the study of the mind. It is not possible to see what is going on in the mind, so psychologists rely on studying the way people behave. This gives them insight into the way the mind works.

Psychiatry is a branch of medicine. Psychiatrists study mental disorders in humans. They try to treat and, if possible, prevent mental health problems. They look at how human behavior changes when the balance of the mind is altered, and try to find ways to help people maintain healthy minds and behaviors.

Normal Behavior and Infant Care

In the 1950s and '60s, American psychologist Harry Harlow carried out work on baby monkeys. At the time, it was thought that children bonded to their mothers because their mothers fed them. Baby rhesus monkeys were taken from their mothers and put in cages. In each cage were two fake mothers. One was made of wire and provided a bottle of milk. The other had no milk, but was covered in warm, cuddly material. The babies spent as little time as possible on the wire mother, only visiting her to feed. They spent most of their time on the cuddly mother. Harlow suggested that cuddling and contact were very important for normal development. The work Harry Harlow carried out on rhesus monkeys showed that interactions with a lot of different animals was important for normal behavior to develop. This also enhanced our knowledge of how human parents and babies interact.

Harry Harlow's experiments demonstrated that young monkeys need their real mothers if they are to develop and behave normally. They also need other monkeys to play and interact with.

Territory, Ownership, and Personal Space

Aggression and display

Animals need space. They need places to raise their young, space to feed, and space to attract a mate. This space is known as their **territory**. Both territory and mates can be in short supply. Many animals show aggressive behavior when they try to gain territory or a mate, and when they want to hold onto them. Food can also be a trigger for aggression. Some animals attack another animal to kill it or to steal its food. Animals can also be aggressive when they defend their food.

Aggression in animals

Aggression is behavior that intimidates, frightens, or hurts another animal. Your pet dog may growl or bark when someone comes to the door. This is threatening behavior—aggression designed to defend the territory. If an animal is badly frightened, it may become aggressive as a form of defense.

In a herd of wild horses or ponies, the stallions (male horses) show aggression and fight each other over ownership of the mares (female horses). The mares can also be aggressive. There is a strict social order, and the **dominant** mares may kick out at lower-ranking horses who do not show enough respect.

Stags fight during the rut (mating season) as they compete for territory and females. This aggression can lead to serious injury and even death.

Reducing the risk

Fighting carries the risk of injury and death. Therefore, many species of animals have developed a less dangerous form of aggressive behavior. Behavioral displays are used to make a point instead of the use of physical violence.

There are many examples of behavior that allow animals to avoid aggression. Marking territory warns other animals that a patch of land is already claimed. Territory marking comes in many forms. It can involve using scent from special glands, urine, or feces. When a pet cat rubs its head against its owner, it is marking and claiming the person as its own. In the same way, a male tiger sprays urine against a tree to tell other male tigers to keep away from his land. Territory marking can also involve sound. Birdsong can be a way of telling other birds to keep away from a particular territory.

Some animals, such as wildebeests and buffalo, form large social herds. Other animals, such as chimpanzees and gorillas, form smaller groups. In these groups there is often a **hierarchy**. The animals at the top got there using very aggressive behavior. However, it would be exhausting and dangerous to be aggressive all the time, and instead very complex social signals have developed. These signals allow the dominant animals to use displays to show that they are at the top. It also means lower-ranking animals can show they accept being less important by displaying to the dominant animals. This means the damage done to individuals is kept to a minimum.

These are some of the signals that animals use to avoid outright aggression.

Human aggression and crime

Aggression in humans includes fighting, road rage, domestic violence, muggings, murder, and war. Many of the triggers for aggressive behavior are similar in humans and animals. In theory, humans are intelligent and can think things through, so there should be less aggression in human society than in animal groups. In fact, aggression is surprisingly common.

Aggressive behavior over territory, belongings, and food is seen in very young children. Adults can have disputes over boundaries that last years. Wars are fought over territory. In this case territory can be land or oil or ideas—but aggression on the level of whole armies is very frightening.

Just like animals, humans have developed many rituals and displays that can be used instead of physical violence. Language means that people can be very aggressive without lifting a finger.

We use signals, such as possessions and lifestyle, to make statements about ourselves. Body language also sends out signals. Smiling, holding doors open, and thousands of other examples of behavior can be used to indicate how dominant we are feeling. Humans avoid aggression by either acknowledging another human's place in the pecking order (their social status), or by asserting their own status in a nonthreatening way.

Crime is often linked with aggression. Why some people become aggressive and/or criminals is not fully understood. Scientists are gathering more and more evidence that both our genetics and our environment affect how aggressive we become.

This graph shows you the trends in recorded violent crime in several countries per 100,000 people between 1962 and 2004. When you remember that the total population of each of these countries runs into millions, you can see that hundreds of thousands of people are the victims of aggressive criminal behavior every year.

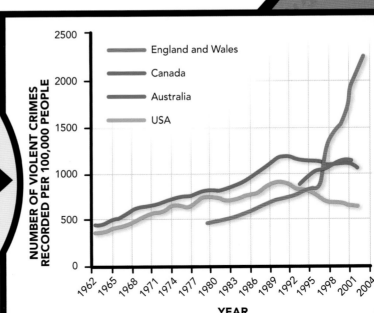

Nature, Nurture, and Criminal Behavior

In the early 21st century, scientists published the results of a study on around 1,000 children in New Zealand taken over a period of 23 years. They were looking for links between genes and upbringing. They measured many things, including the levels of a chemical called **monoamine oxidase (MAOA)**. MAOA breaks down chemical messengers in the brain. High levels of MAOA seem to be linked to depression. Low MAOA levels seem to be linked to aggressive behavior. The level of MAOA someone makes is inherited.

No one has to be a criminal and end up in a prison like this one. However, evidence suggests that the genes we inherit may make some of us more likely to be aggressive and violent than others, and so more likely to commit a crime.

The scientists found a clear **correlation** between the way children coped with being treated badly and their MAOA levels. Those who suffered bad treatment as children, but had high MAOA levels were no more likely to be violent or criminal than anyone else. However, those who had low MAOA levels and were badly treated seemed to be worse affected. They only made up 12 percent of the group, but they made up 44 percent of the people convicted of violent crime.

The gene for MAOA is inherited on the chromosomes that determine gender, and problems are more common in men. This may help explain why males are more likely than females to be involved in aggressive and criminal behavior. The evidence from this study suggests that an interaction between genes (the level of MAOA in the brain) and environment (whether or not someone is badly treated as a child) may affect how aggressive a person is as an adult.

Human Behavior Throughout Life

The early years

When human babies are born, they are completely dependent on adults to look after them. Without this care the baby will die. The behavior of babies is largely the result of reflex responses and instincts. Some behaviors are simple reflexes, such as the rooting response. When its face is touched, the baby turns its head and opens its mouth to search for food. Other simple patterns of behavior encourage parents to respond to and look after their baby. They are known as signaling behaviors because they send clear signals to the carers. When a baby is hungry, cold, or unhappy, it will cry. When someone comforts or feeds the baby, the crying stops. Evidence suggests that when carers respond quickly to a crying baby, the baby cries less. It soon learns to trust that help will come when it is needed.

Crying is an instinctive behavior in small babies. It causes strong responses in adults, which encourages them to look after the baby.

CUTTING EDGE: THE PHYSICAL RESPONSE TO CRYING

The sound of a baby crying has a physical effect on adults, whether they are parents or not. American scientist Ann Frodi at the University of Rochester has carried out tests on the effect of crying on parents, childless adults, teenagers, and even children as young as eight years old.

When they heard a baby crying, they all showed an increase in heart rate and blood pressure and a change in the way their skin conducts electricity. Everyone described anxiety and irritation at the sound, and a desire to make it stop.

How does behavior develop?

The way children learn to behave depends on a number of things. Teaching and learning is very important. Parents, grandparents, other carers, teachers at school, and even older brothers and sisters all teach a child how to behave. These lessons vary from simply learning the skills needed to look after yourself—bowel and bladder control, teeth cleaning, and how to put on shoes—to good manners, cooperation, and self-control.

One important way in which children learn is through observation and copying. It is not just simple behaviors that are copied. Children learn morals from their parents from a very early age. For example, children from a considerate home are likely to be thoughtful of others, whereas children who see violence are more likely to lash out to solve their own problems.

Mimicry (copying) plays a big part in the way children learn to behave.

Toddlers and children

As babies grow into toddlers, and toddlers grow into children, behavior changes from instincts and reflexes to more learned and conscious behavior. The development of social skills is an important area of behavior. If a child learns to interact happily with its carers, other adults, and other children, it will have the foundation for mental and physical health and stability.

Adolescence to adulthood

The behavior of children affects their health. Children are naturally inquisitive and active, busy playing and exploring their environment. However, more and more children in the United States spend a lot of time watching television and playing computer games. The food they eat is often high in fats and sugars. As a result, an increasing number of children are becoming overweight or obese. This has a direct effect on their health. They become breathless easily and are more likely to suffer from asthma and diabetes. In the future they may be more likely to develop heart disease and some cancers.

 THE SCIENCE YOU LEARN: CHANGES AT PUBERTY

At puberty, the brain and sex organs (ovaries in girls, testes in boys) start to make chemical messages known as sex **hormones**. These hormones trigger all the other physical changes that occur at puberty, which include growth, change in body shape, the start of periods (menstruation) in girls, and the production of sperm in boys.

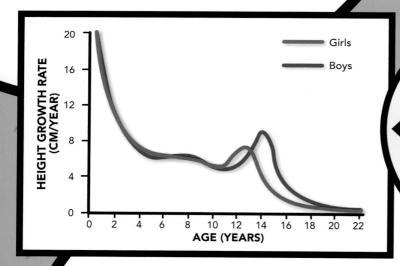

Your growth rate is fastest when you are a baby. It slows down a lot by the time you are about three years old. During puberty your growth rate increases, as you grow from a child to an adult.

The behavior of adolescents shows some clearly-defined patterns. Teenagers find it harder to get to sleep. They often go to bed later, but since they are growing fast they need a lot of sleep. As a result they tend to wake up late and groggy in the mornings. Peer-group relationships become more and more important as teenagers distance themselves from family ties. They become more independent. At this point real dangers can appear. Binge drinking, drug taking, and violent behavior are increasingly seen in teenagers, and often peer pressure is part of the problem. Behavior like this can have serious health consequences in both the short and the long term (see pages 44–47).

Teenagers can also have problems with empathy, which means they find it difficult to understand the points of view of other people. Yet they can also be caring, compassionate, and idealistic. While teenagers can experience powerful mood swings as a result of the brain restructuring that is going on, they find it more difficult to recognize emotions in other people.

Sexual behavior is an important part of adolescent development. The sexes become much more aware of each other. Finding a boyfriend or girlfriend and sexual behavior take up increasing amounts of time and thought.

In a teenager's brain, many different nerve connections are being removed or reformed. In particular, changes take place in parts of the brain concerned with emotion and motivation. The teenage brain can have real problems in assessing risks. The risky, daredevil behavior of some young people is often seen as rebellion or wildness. It may simply be an inability to make the connection between behavior, such as driving recklessly or drug taking, and the possible consequences.

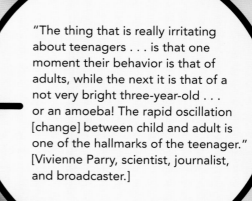

"The thing that is really irritating about teenagers . . . is that one moment their behavior is that of adults, while the next it is that of a not very bright three-year-old . . . or an amoeba! The rapid oscillation [change] between child and adult is one of the hallmarks of the teenager." [Vivienne Parry, scientist, journalist, and broadcaster.]

Adulthood and old age

Human adult behavior is extremely varied. This is partly because adult behavior depends strongly on the culture to which a person belongs. The behavior of adult women in an American city will be very different from the behavior of adult women in a remote village in India, for example. Masai warriors in Africa will behave very differently from U.S. farmers. Many of these differences are examples of learned behavior. Children born in one community, but raised in the traditions of another, will show the behavior patterns of the place where they grew up.

Some types of behavior are common to adults in almost every culture. Sexual behavior is one (see pages 32–37). Parenting behavior is another. The details of parenting behavior vary among cultures, but there are some common threads. Mothers usually nurture their children. They either breast-feed their infants or use a bottle with artificial milk formula. In many cultures women do most of the child rearing, so much of the behavior learned by very young children comes from their mothers. The role of fathers in raising children varies widely across cultures. A very involved approach is encouraged in the United States at the moment, but in other communities, men take little or no part in raising their children.

Adults usually work, either for money or to maintain a home and feed a family. Adult behavior also involves self-control, the ability to empathize with others, and the ability to plan and take charge. In adult communities, some people are more dominant than others. This can be seen clearly in the workplace, and sometimes in the home.

The choices adults make about their behavior in everyday life—the food they eat, what they drink, how much they exercise, and whether they smoke or use drugs—all have a big effect on their health and well-being (see pages 42–47).

Aging

As humans age, physical changes can affect the way they behave. Muscles weaken, eyesight and hearing worsen, healing takes longer, and memory may begin to fail. All of these things can reduce a person's confidence and affect the way they behave. People may be just as capable of enjoying a game of basketball when they are 70 years old as when they were 40, or even 20. But the fear of injury, or of not seeing the ball clearly, often means that older people withdraw from sports and other activities. Yet maintaining normal active behavior is one of the most important ways to stay healthy into old age. It keeps the muscles as strong as possible and reduces the chance of heart disease. Staying active also helps people keep their weight down and makes them less likely to have diseases, such as diabetes and arthritis. Enjoying life and staying mentally active helps reduce the likelihood of memory loss or depression.

Behavior changes dramatically at different stages of life. At every stage, behavior has an effect on our health.

Sexual Behavior

Courtship and mating in the animal world

Many animals do not mate. Instead they release their sex cells into water. Animals that live on land have to mate to pass the male sex cells into the female body to meet the egg. In many animals, finding a partner and mating involves some very complex behavior. Most of this behavior is instinctive or innate rather than learned, although most animals get better at it with practice.

Courtship displays

Male and female animals, including humans, are often looking for different things when it comes to reproduction. Males make huge quantities of very small sex cells. They want to mate with many females and father as many offspring as possible. Females make a limited number of much larger sex (egg) cells. It takes a lot of resources to make eggs and a big investment of time in the developing young. Therefore, females look for a small number of partners, but they are looking for the best possible mates. They need the best genetic material so their offspring have a good chance of survival. A mate with control of a large territory means there will be plenty of food for the offspring. A mate who will help to rear the young means the offspring are more likely to survive.

Many animals have courtship rituals, where the males display in some way and the females choose their mates. Courtship displays may rely on sight and/or sound. Many also depend on scent. Chemicals called **pheromones** are produced, and these attract the opposite sex. Unlike humans, most female animals are only prepared to mate when they are fertile, so male animals also rely on scent to tell them when a female is ready to mate.

The dangers of mating

Once courtship is over and a mate is chosen, the animals will mate. This can be very dangerous. For many female animals it means allowing another potentially dangerous animal to come extremely close to you. She will be within easy reach of claws, jaws, and teeth. For this reason, during mating some animals like to make sure that their partner is occupied and already has something to eat. Praying mantises and a number of spiders famously eat their mates during the act of mating unless they are successfully distracted.

Animal Courtship Rituals

In some species of hangingflies, the males offer the females a dead insect to eat while mating. This proves they are good providers. The bigger the dead insect, the longer the female will mate, and the more eggs the male can fertilize.

Male birds of paradise have beautiful feathers and often perform complicated mating dances. They use the dances to display their feathers to attract a female.

The fights between male elephant seals for territory and females can leave both animals injured, and many seal pups are crushed during the battle.

The display of a male bird of paradise is designed to convince a female that he would be a good father for her offspring.

Human sexual behavior

Just like other animals, human sexual behavior is all about attracting a mate. Unlike many other animals, humans can choose to be sexually active at any point during the menstrual cycle.

Sexual behavior is not simple. It is a mixture of innate patterns caused by hormones inside the body, responses to signals from other humans, and learned behavior. Humans learn about sexual behavior by watching and listening to others, from characters in films to their parents.

Human displays

In many ways, human courtship is very different from animals because we use the higher centers of our brain and think carefully about what we are doing. Humans live as part of a society, and a mate who is well regarded in society is very valuable. In many human societies, sex is closely linked to marriage, when a man and a woman form a partnership. However, when it comes to sex, in some ways we are still very much like animals and respond strongly to certain signals.

Some of the signals that humans respond to are obvious. Appearance is very important in human sexual behavior. This is why humans dress up for a night out! The way humans speak and the things they say are also important. Scent is another important aspect of human sexual behavior, which is why perfume, deodorant, and aftershave sell so well. There are also other more subtle scents that our bodies respond to. Humans produce pheromones and detect these signals. In one piece of research, scientists sprayed male pheromones on certain chairs in a waiting room. Later, women only sat on the sprayed chairs. When the situation was reversed and female pheromones were used, men actively chose to sit on the sprayed chairs. Without any awareness of what was going on, people chose the chairs that gave out a message about sex!

The Power of Advertising

The sex drive in humans is very strong. In men, the sight of an attractive woman can very rapidly arouse desire. In women, the situation is more complex, although physical appearance is important. The advertising and marketing industries use these responses because using sex in advertisements sells products. This is partly because the images make people take notice of the ad. The images also suggest that if you use a certain product, you too will be sexually successful. In advertising directed at men, beautiful women are often involved. The subtle message is: Buy this product and you will attract beautiful women. In advertising that targets women, good-looking men and romance are often featured. The biological message that works for women is: Buy this product and you will attract good-looking, rich, successful men who will father healthy children and help you take care of them!

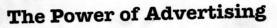

Sexual behavior in humans, from a Valentine's day dinner to an expensive wedding, is part of a huge industry. Yet in biological terms, sexual behavior is still all about selecting a mate and producing healthy babies.

Sexual health

Humans do not have sexual intercourse only to conceive offspring. In fact, many do not want to get pregnant every time they have sex. One important form of human sexual behavior is the use of **contraception**. Contraception literally means against conception. Barrier methods of contraception, such as the condom, stop the sperm from reaching the egg. The birth control pill is a chemical method of contraception.

Irresponsible sexual behavior can lead to a number of different sexually transmitted diseases. HIV/AIDS is caused by the viruses you can see here attacking a white blood cell. There is still no cure for this disease.

Sexually transmitted diseases

One result of human sexual behavior is the spread of **sexually transmitted diseases (STDs)**. An STD is passed from one person to another through sexual activity. Anyone who is sexually active can catch an STD.

In their early stages, STDs most commonly affect the sex organs. In many cases, untreated STDs can cause **infertility**. Some, like syphilis, can cause serious illness and death. The human papilloma virus causes genital warts. These affect men and women and are unpleasant, but not usually serious. However, the same virus has also been shown to cause cervical cancer in women. This cancer can be treated successfully if it is discovered early, but thousands of women still die from it every year. A vaccine is now available, which can be given to young women before they become sexually active to help protect them from the virus.

Perhaps the best-known result of dangerous sexual behavior is HIV/AIDS, a viral disease that attacks the body's defense system. So far, although new medicines can help people live much longer, there is no cure or vaccine for this disease.

Most STDs can be treated, and if they are caught early they have no long-term effects. Unfortunately it is not easy to tell if someone has an STD. Many STDs do not cause major symptoms for years, and if someone catches one it is easy to miss the early symptoms. Humans can carry an STD for years, passing it on to their sexual partners until they become seriously ill or realize they are infertile. Sensible sexual behavior is vital to avoid the problems of STDs. That includes having only one sexual partner and using barrier contraception with a new partner. Ideally, barrier methods of contraception should continue to be used until both partners have had tests to show that they are free from STDs.

SCIENCE YOU LEARN: CONCEPTION TO BIRTH

During sexual intercourse, the male sperm (sex cells) are released inside the body of the female. They move through the uterus into the fallopian tubes. If an egg (the female sex cell) has been released from the ovary, the sperm will cluster around the egg. Eventually one sperm may penetrate the protective coating of the egg. This is the moment of conception, when a potential new life begins. The fertilized egg begins to divide and over nine months becomes a fully developed baby.

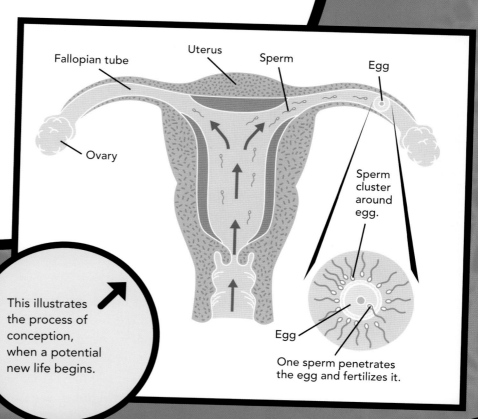

Fallopian tube

Uterus

Sperm

Egg

Ovary

Sperm cluster around egg.

Egg

One sperm penetrates the egg and fertilizes it.

This illustrates the process of conception, when a potential new life begins.

Health and Behavior

Eating too much—or too little

In places such as the United States, Europe, and Australia there is plenty of food, much of it cheap and often high in calories. Many people eat a healthy, balanced diet, but eating behavior is changing. The modern trend is to graze throughout the day on high-energy snacks, coffee, and fast food. As a result, people are getting fatter. There is good scientific evidence that increasing weight is linked to health problems, such as heart disease and diabetes.

Unhealthy eating habits can seriously affect your health and well-being.

Some people eat too much, but others eat too little. Eating behavior becomes distorted when people deliberately starve themselves. This eating disorder is called anorexia nervosa. Eating disorders are mental illnesses in which people perceive themselves as fat even when they are dangerously thin. They feel they need to control everything that goes into and out of the body.

Does food affect health?

There is increasing evidence that a diet high in fruit and vegetables can help protect you against heart disease and a number of different cancers. A diet that is high in animal fats, such as butter and cream, seems to be linked to an increased risk of heart disease and cancers. The amount of salt in your diet can affect your blood pressure, although only some people are sensitive to salt levels. There is still a lot to discover about the links between eating behavior and health. How do scientists find out what is going on?

INVESTIGATION PANEL: LOOKING FOR CAUSE AND EFFECT

Finding out how human behavior affects health is not easy. You cannot easily experiment on humans. To show that a particular behavior causes certain health effects, scientists need to look at data (information) from thousands of people. For example, The National Children's Study has been set up in the United States. The aim is to investigate genetic influences and environmental influences, such as diet, social setting, and education, on children's health and well-being. Much of the funding is coming from the United States government.

More than 100,000 children will be observed in 105 different study centers. The children will come from across the United States so that every different ethnic group is included. The children will be observed from before birth (when their mothers are pregnant) until they are 21 years old.

Scientists will collect the information through interviews with the mothers, and with the children as they get older. They will also use questionnaires and examine the health and development of the children at regular intervals. At the end of the study, scientists hope to identify which factors in the behavior of pregnant women and in the way children are fed and brought up help to make them healthier for the rest of their lives.

Similar studies have been carried out and are happening in many other countries.

Stress, exercise, and health

Modern life is very busy. In school there is constant pressure to achieve and fit in. For adults there are the demands of work, home, family, and friends. Most of the time, these stresses are a good thing. They lend a sense of purpose, excitement, and challenge. However, sometimes the pressure is too much, or goes on for too long. Then it can lead to illness, with both physical and emotional problems. Millions of people visit their doctor each year with stress-related problems.

For severe problems a doctor will prescribe medicine, but many people manage to overcome their stress without drugs. They may go on vacation, or take up a relaxing hobby. A lot of people take up exercise, from yoga to running. Exercise relieves stress. It is physically demanding and takes your mind off the stress. It is tiring, which is why it helps people to sleep. Exercise also triggers the release of feel-good chemicals in the brain, known as endorphins, which can cause feelings of happiness.

Exercise is good for both your mental and physical health. →

Exercise and health

Exercise is also important for good health in many other ways. A lot of people get very little exercise. They may prefer to watch television or use the computer. Yet scientific evidence shows that people who exercise regularly are healthier. They are less likely to be affected by heart disease and a disease called osteoporosis, in which the bones become easy to break.

INVESTIGATION PANEL: HOW MUCH EXERCISE DO YOU DO?

Investigate the exercise levels in your local community, whether in school or at home.

Procedure

1. Write a short questionnaire designed to find out how much exercise people do. Reassure people that the questionnaire will be anonymous. Choose your questions carefully. Just asking "Do you exercise?" will not tell you much. Useful questions include "How many times do you exercise for more than 20 minutes each week?" and "Do you walk or cycle to work?" Record the age and sex of the people who complete your questionnaire.

2. Decide how many questionnaires you are going to use. The more you fill in, the more reliable your results will be, but the more data you will have to deal with. Hand out your questionnaires.

3. Analyze the data you have collected. For example, you could produce a bar chart to show the number of times people exercise in a week. You could draw a pie chart to show the percentage of people who walk or cycle to work or school compared to those taking the bus, a car, or a train (depending on where you live).

4. Look at your data and draw conclusions about the activity levels of the people you have studied. Are they active and healthy, or do they need to do more exercise? If they need to do more, how could a person persuade them to do so?

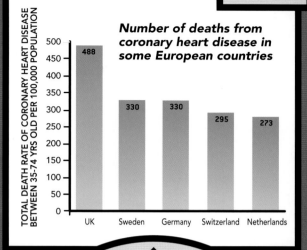

Graph A

Number of deaths from coronary heart disease in some European countries

Graph A shows the number of deaths from heart disease in several European countries. Graph B shows the percentage of journeys made by bicycle in the same countries. This gives a good idea of the level of exercise people do. There seems to be a link between exercise and heart health, although one piece of evidence does not prove or disprove a theory.

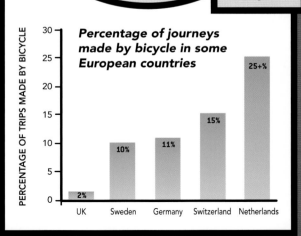

Graph B

Percentage of journeys made by bicycle in some European countries

Legal drugs, legal killers

A drug is a chemical that has a specific effect on your body. Many drugs are prescribed by doctors to help the body overcome diseases. Some, like minor painkillers and indigestion tablets, are sold over the counter at drugstores.

Tea, coffee, cigarettes, and alcoholic drinks contain legal and commonly used drugs, but there are other drugs that are not legal to use. To make the right decisions about using legal and illegal drugs, it is important to realize that both can damage health. In the United States, 100,000 deaths occur each year from the effects of alcohol, and another 400,000 occur from smoking-related diseases.

Smoking is a behavior that has well-known negative effects on your health and appearance, yet millions of people continue to smoke.

Smoking

Around the world, millions of people smoke tobacco, most commonly as cigarettes. Cigarette smoke contains many different chemicals, including a drug called nicotine. This drug stimulates the body but narrows the blood vessels. It makes people feel calmer and more able to cope with stress. However, the body becomes addicted to nicotine. As people get used to the drug, they need more nicotine to have the same effect, and therefore smoke more cigarettes.

Cigarette smoke also contains a thick black tar that builds up in the lungs. This tar makes smokers more likely to get bronchitis and other serious lung conditions. Smoking is also strongly linked to lung cancer. Up to 90 percent of all cases of lung cancer are caused by smoking. The heart is also affected by smoking, making a heart attack or stroke far more likely. Smoking ages the skin, and women who smoke when they are pregnant increase the risk of their babies dying.

Sir Richard Doll

Richard Doll was a British scientist who researched the link between smoking and lung cancer. He is famous for being the first person ever to provide a scientific link between the two. He worked at the United Kingdom Medical Research Council and published his groundbreaking paper in 1954. He gave up smoking himself during his study. Since then, thousands of studies have confirmed the links between smoking and many different health problems. Sir Richard Doll himself went on to study smoking-related diseases for more than 50 years.

Data like this has been collected over many years. The evidence against cigarettes is overwhelming.

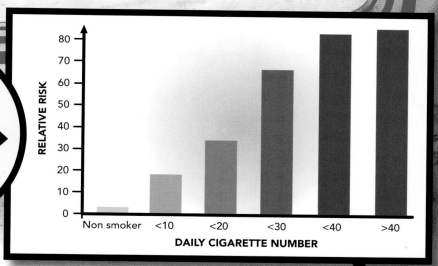

Why smoke?

Most people begin smoking when they are fairly young. They may copy their parents, or start to smoke because it is regarded as cool or rebellious. Yet other young people start to smoke as a result of pressure from their peer group—if your friends smoke, it can be hard to say no. Whatever the reasons for starting, the reason people continue to smoke is their addiction to nicotine. This is what makes it so hard to change smoking behavior. It is far better not to start.

Alcohol—legal but dangerous

Alcohol is a social drug that is widely used in many parts of the world. When someone drinks an alcoholic drink, the alcohol passes into the bloodstream and into almost every tissue of the body, including the brain. It slows down thought processes and reflexes. All reactions become slower than normal.

A little alcohol can make people feel relaxed and at ease. It also leads to a lack of self control and a lack of judgment. More alcohol can cause aggression and a complete loss of control. The person may pass out and even die.

Alcohol is addictive. When people cannot cope without alcohol they are called alcoholics. Heavy alcohol use over a period of years can cause long-term damage to the brain. The brains of dead alcoholics are sometimes so soft and pulpy that almost all of the normal brain structures have been lost.

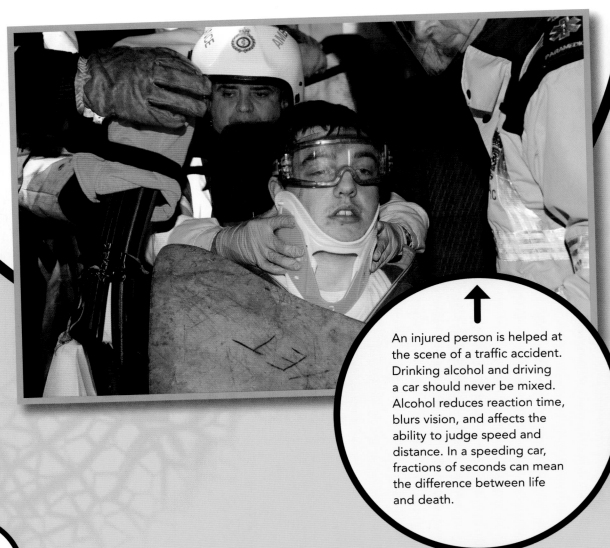

An injured person is helped at the scene of a traffic accident. Drinking alcohol and driving a car should never be mixed. Alcohol reduces reaction time, blurs vision, and affects the ability to judge speed and distance. In a speeding car, fractions of seconds can mean the difference between life and death.

Normally alcohol is broken down in the liver into harmless substances. People who drink very large amounts of alcohol, or who drink heavily for a long time, are at risk from potentially fatal liver diseases. These include cirrhosis of the liver and liver cancer.

Many nondrinkers also suffer from alcohol abuse. Drunk drivers kill people in road accidents. Violent crimes are committed after drinking. Families can break down as a result of one or both parents drinking heavily. If pregnant women drink too much alcohol, their baby may be born with disabilities.

People have drunk alcoholic drinks for centuries, but if the drug was discovered today it would probably be banned as too dangerous for use.

Binge Drinking

Excessive alcohol consumption with the main purpose of getting drunk is called binge drinking. This has become a major problem in many countries of the world.

In the United States, there are laws in every state that make it illegal for anyone under the age of 21 to purchase or possess alcohol. However, young people report that alcohol is easy to obtain. According to the U.S. Department of Health and Human Services, over 10 million adolescents from 12 to 20 admit to using alcohol. Of those, over 5 million are binge drinkers. Frequent binge drinkers are eight times more likely to miss a class, fall behind in schoolwork, get hurt or injured, and damage property.

At college age the statistics get even worse. According to a 1997 national study conducted by Harvard School of Public Health, nearly half of all college students surveyed binge drank within the previous two weeks. Binge drinking during college may be associated with mental health disorders such as compulsiveness, depression, and anxiety. Over half of the college students who are frequent binge drinkers also admit that they drink and drive.

The U.S. and other countries are looking for ways to control this problem. They want to prevent the damage caused to individuals and society before it is too late.

Illegal drugs

Many illegal drugs have a powerful effect on the mind. Some produce hallucinations (like waking dreams). Others give the user an overwhelming sense of happiness and power. Once people have experienced the drug's high, they want it again and again. Addicts may not be able to cope with life without the drug. It is very difficult to stop using drugs. If people give up the drug, they feel extremely ill as they suffer from withdrawal symptoms.

Most illegal drugs can damage your health by causing heart failure and death. This can happen the first time you try a drug, or the 100th time. Illegal drugs are expensive. Addicts often get involved in crime to pay for their drugs. Many addicts damage their health because they live in great poverty. They spend all their money on drugs, rather than eating a balanced diet or staying clean.

Spreading disease

Some drugs are injected straight into the bloodstream. Once addicts start injecting drugs, they may share needles with other drug users. Serious diseases can be spread in this way. Blood infected with microbes can be passed from one person to another on dirty needles. Hepatitis, a serious disease of the liver, and HIV/AIDS are common among injecting drug addicts. In addition, if people are caught using or supplying illegal drugs, they can be tried and sent to prison. In some parts of the world they are even put to death.

So far, science has not found a way to overcome the cravings of a drug addict. There is relatively little money available to support research. The behavior of an addict almost always damages their health, but the behavior needed to overcome the addiction takes a lot of character and determination. Many people find this very hard.

Crystal Meth

Crystal meth (methamphetamine) is a relatively new and inexpensive drug. It is snorted up the nose, injected, or smoked, and it acts as a stimulant. People feel high, very awake, alert, and happy for hours after using the drug. It also tends to make people very sexually active.

Crystal meth is also very destructive. It can have a very rapid damaging effect on both health and behavior. It is psychologically very addictive, and it affects mental health and well-being. It can cause mood swings, paranoia, rage, and short-term memory loss. It damages the mouth and skin, leading to horrible sores. If people overdose on the drug, they can suffer a complete collapse of their circulatory and breathing systems, go into a coma, and die. People using crystal meth often also have a lot of sex with a lot of different people, putting them at risk of STDs. In the United States, for example, almost 50 percent of new cases of HIV/AIDS involve the use of crystal meth.

The use of crystal meth is spreading from the United States to many other countries.

These two photos of the same crystal meth addict were taken 18 months apart. The more recent photograph on the right clearly shows the woman's worsening physical condition.

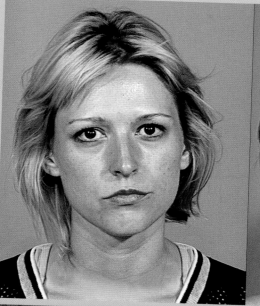
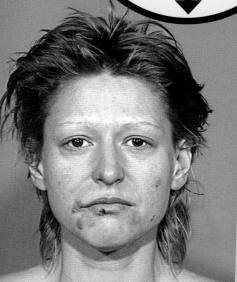

Summary

Health and behavior

Behavior is the actions displayed by an organism in response to its environment. Behavior is affected by factors inside and outside the body, and can be observed and measured. Animal behavior involves everything that goes on in life, from eating and defending territories to raising young. It ranges from simple reflexes to complicated human actions, such as developing the technology to send people into space.

In humans and many other larger animals, behavior depends on three things. The senses provide information about the outside world and the inside of the body, the central nervous system analyzes the information, and nerves send messages out to the muscles, controlling movement.

The study of animal behavior has taught us a great deal about the basis of human behavior. Although much of human behavior depends on conscious thought, instinct and innate behavior are also very involved in life. There are ethical problems with experimenting on humans, so a lot of work on human behavior is carried out using large surveys. It is interesting to see how much of our behavior is part of our genetic makeup, and how much is a result of the environment in which we grow up.

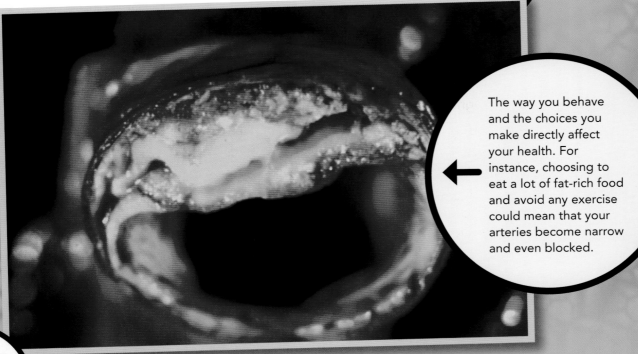

The way you behave and the choices you make directly affect your health. For instance, choosing to eat a lot of fat-rich food and avoid any exercise could mean that your arteries become narrow and even blocked.

Health and behavior go hand in hand for individuals, families, and the whole community. This is why understanding human behavior and the way it affects your health matters so much.

There is no doubt that the way you behave affects your health. Your behavior and responses change as you grow. A newborn baby is all reflexes, but much adult behavior is the result of conscious thought. Some human behaviors, such as aggressive tendencies, have their roots in animal behavior. Since people can think things through, these behaviors are often changed and used in different ways.

The food you choose to eat also has a major effect on your health. Too much food, too little, a lot of fat, a lot of fruit—all can affect the health of your body.

Like all animals, one of the strongest drives in human behavior is the desire to find a mate and produce offspring. Sexual behavior also carries with it the risk of unwanted pregnancy and STDs.

Once people have children, parenting behavior becomes very important if the baby is to grow up happy and secure. However, it is not just upbringing that affects a child. As children grow up, the influence of their peer group becomes a big factor in the way they behave. Peer groups often influence whether people start smoking, drinking, or using illegal drugs. These chemicals affect the brain and alter behavior. They can have devastating effects on health and well-being.

Many people don't know how much their behavior affects their mental and physical health, but once you are aware, you can begin to make choices that will keep you as healthy as possible.

Facts and Figures

Timeline of the study of behavior

350 BCE Greek philosopher Aristotle writes about memory and reminiscence as he tries to explain how people remember things.

1566 CE The Spaniard Bernardino Alvarez sets up the Hospital do San Hipolito in Mexico, the first hospital in the Americas for patients with mental health problems.

1791 Italian scientist Luigi Galvani uses the muscles in frogs' legs to show that nerve impulses are electrical.

1875 British scientist Francis Galton (Darwin's cousin) introduces the use of twins in studies in his book *History of Twins*.

1877 Charles Darwin, the great British scientist, publishes *Sketch of an Infant*, a detailed account of the development and behavior of one of his own children.

1906 Russian scientist Ivan Pavlov publishes his famous experiments on conditioned reflexes in dogs.

1930s–'50s Burrhus Skinner carries out his work on conditioning in rats and pigeons, and many other aspects of behavior.

1950s Konrad Lorenz (Austrian) and Nikolaas Tinbergen (Dutch), with Karl von Frisch (Austrian), develop the science of ethology, the study of animal behavior in natural contexts.

1950s–'60s American psychologist Harry Harlow carries out experiments on the mother-infant bond in rhesus monkeys.

1962–63 The first evidence is uncovered that physical changes in the brain take place when something is memorized.

1960s–'70s Scientists Jane Goodall and Dian Fossey study the behavior of chimpanzees and mountain gorillas, respectively.

1990s MRI scanning becomes available, allowing scientists to see what is happening inside the brain.

2002 Studies show how inherited levels of MAOA interact with the childhood environment to influence behavior.

2007 Work in the United Kingdom and elsewhere suggests that some people resist peer pressure more easily than others.

Biographies

Burrhus Frederic Skinner

Born in 1904 in Pennsylvania, Burrhus Frederic Skinner studied English literature before he became involved in animal behavior. Burrhus had always enjoyed building things, and he quickly began to devise new apparatuses for his investigations. It wasn't long before his famous Skinner box was produced (see page 12). By 1938 he had published his first book on behavior. During World War II (1939–1945), Skinner worked on a top-secret project, training pigeons to guide bombs.

In 1948 he joined the Psychology Department at Harvard University and stayed there for the rest of his working life. He also became involved in education after he discovered that the way children were taught math went against everything he had discovered about the way animals learn. He spent many years developing improved ways of teaching children in schools. Skinner died of leukemia in 1990.

Dame Jane Goodall

Jane Goodall was born in London in 1934. She is one of the best-known ethologists and primatologists (people who study primates). She studied at Cambridge University, and then worked with the anthropologist Louis Leakey and his wife Henrietta when they were searching for early human remains in Africa. Leakey was very impressed with Jane and asked her to study the chimpanzees of Gombe Stream National Park in Tanzania. She came back to England to complete her PhD, and from then on the focus of her work was Gombe.

Goodall's detailed observations of chimpanzee behavior allowed scientists to build up a picture of the way individuals interact, and the way aggressive behavior builds up and is dealt with. Her studies have helped push forward the boundaries of knowledge on both chimp and human behavior. She is also actively involved in conservation work.

Find Out More

Books

Cash, Adam. *Psychology for Dummies.* Indianapolis, IN: Wiley Publishing, 2002.

Fullick, Ann. *Life Science In Depth: Body Systems and Health.* Chicago: Heinemann Library, 2006.

Green, Christopher. *Toddler Taming: A Survival Guide for Parents.* New York: Ballantine Books, 1985.

Websites

http://www.abovetheinfluence.com/
Read about the dangers of alcohol and drugs and increase your awareness of the influences around you.

http://nobelprize.org/educational_games/medicine/pavlov/readmore.html
Find out all about the work of Pavlov and his dogs.

http://nobelprize.org/educational_games/medicine/split-brain
Play this game to help you understand how the different areas of your brain work.

http://smoking.drugabuse.gov/
Learn more about the health risks of nicotine and other drugs, and find links to other useful sites and information.

http://kidshealth.org/teen/drug_alcohol/alcohol/alcohol.html
Find information on drinking and alcohol use and abuse, and how it can affect teenagers.

http://www.parenting.org/
Find parenting help, including advice and further resources.

Topics for further study

- Biruté Galdikas and her orangutan studies.

- Dian Fossey and her work with mountain gorillas.

- Konrad Lorenz and his geese.

- Sigmund Freud and psychoanalysis.

- Harry Harlow and his baby rhesus monkeys.

- The development of language in chimpanzees.

- Piaget and his work on child development.

- The Stanford Prison Experiment.
  This is a famous experiment on how people behave when they are put in a position of power, and how they behave as prisoners. (www.prisonexp.org)

- Ways to change behavior for the better.
  Investigate ways to reduce or stop drinking or smoking. Find out which methods are the most successful and why.

Glossary

aggression behavior that intimidates, frightens, or hurts another animal or person

chromosome structure found in all living cells that carries genetic information

conditioned reflex reflex learned through repeating an action

contraception prevention of sperm from meeting a fertile egg

correlation linked relationship between two different factors

culture shared system of beliefs, attitudes, and values of a group of people

DNA (deoxyribonucleic acid) material that forms the genetic information in the cells

dominant organism at the top of the social order in a group

ethical issue issue in which there is an element of right and wrong, good or bad, which depends on the views of an individual or society as a whole

ethologist scientist who studies the behavior of animals, particularly when they are in their natural environment

ethology the study of animal behavior, particularly in the natural environment

evaluate assess the strengths and weaknesses of an investigation

gene section of DNA that is the basic unit of inheritance

hierarchy ranking of individuals in a social group or herd

hormone chemical produced in the body that controls specific actions. Sex hormones control sexual development.

infertility being unable to produce offspring

innate behavior that is preprogrammed and does not have to be learned

instinct behavior that is preprogrammed and does not have to be learned

longitudinal study series of observations carried out on the same people over many years

monoamine oxidase (MAOA)   chemical that breaks down chemical messages in the brain

MRI (magnetic resonance imaging) scanner   scanner that produces an image of the molecules that make up a substance. It is very useful for seeing the soft tissues of the human body, such as the brain.

nerve impulse   electrical message that travels through the nervous system

neuroscientist   scientist who studies the nervous system

obese   very overweight

pheromone   chemical produced by an animal that influences the behavior or development of another animal of the same species

psychiatry   branch of medicine involving the treatment of mental health problems

psychology   study of the mind, based on behavior

sense organ   organ that is sensitive to a stimulus such as sight, sound, or smell

sensitivity   awareness to a change in the environment

sexually transmitted disease (STD)   disease that is passed from one person to another through sexual contact

stimulus   something that causes a response in a body part or organ, for example, a pin prick or a sound

territory   area that an animal, pair of animals, or group of animals defends

Index